Ar ... Our
Love
The Rest is our Secret

Helena Guerreiro-Klinowski

An Iota of Our Love
The Rest is Our Secret

By Helena Guerreiro-Klinowski

ISBN: 13:978-1480037397

Designer: Anton Botha of SBRM | www.sbrm.com

Publisher/Editor: Caterina Mecca Patel

Cover Art Acknowledgement:
The painting on the covers is by Émile Klinowski.

For my

Soulmate, Lover, Husband, Friend

Émile Klinowski

I love you
yesterday
today
and always

You are the
purpose
soul
meaning
whole
of my life!

Contents

Introduction

A life is a burst of energy, a surge of potential that seeks fulfillment and soon ebbs into the mystery from whence it came. It is a quivering flame, fragile and easily extinguishable; a wind that blows for awhile and then is still; a swell that forms into a wave and crashes onto the shore to be reabsorbed by the ocean.

From the context of the Universe we are a microcosmic experience. From our own context we are the centre of the Universe, all important and masterful. We are often confronted with death through the tragedies of others who succumb to illness, accidents or become the victims of war. These occurrences are perceived as happening to others only and seldom awaken an awareness of the fragility and insignificance of our own lives. We continue to reinforce our illusion of invulnerability.

We may empathize with the pain and suffering of others, with their losses and the collapse of their world. We may offer words of comfort and provide support in a myriad of ways but through it all we remain external to their experiences. Our life continues with the same rhythm as before. There are dreams to be fulfilled, successes to be attained, things to be acquired, desires to be quenched, sights to be seen, knowledge to be absorbed, emotions to be explored, adventures to be sought. There are also problems to be solved, turmoils to be resolved, obstacles to be overcome, fears to be conquered, debts to be paid. We follow the flow of our own existence and expect others to do likewise, including those at the centre of their tragedies. After all, "Time heals all wounds" and "Life goes on".

What if by some cruel circumstance we were to find ourselves suddenly in the midst of a shattering experience. What if the horror and tragedy happened to us and we witnessed the collapse of our own individual world. Then, and only then, would we realize in the innermost part of our being, that this irrevocable event had changed everything. What was, ceases to be. The flow of life becomes dammed. The mundane seems absurd and irrelevant. All is filtered through a different prism as a result of this mega shift in one's life. Then, and only then, would we realize that time does not heal all wounds and life can come to a stop even when we are alive. I know. My life came to a stop after a sudden moment on November 23, 1993 when my Great Love, Émile Klinowski died. The pain still prevails.

When Émile and I met, we each immediately recognized the soulmate in the other. Intuitively we knew that the depth and intensity of our love had roots beyond time and space. On October 27, 1979 our lives were united in marriage. During fourteen years and twenty-seven days of blissful love, flying adventures, travels and challenges, we thrived in each other's company.

One day, a little lost blue tabby cat found his way to our home and hearts. We called him Perdu. He became an inseparable loving family member. The three of us lived in Schomberg, our Shangri-la. On May 3, 1992 Émile experienced a sudden heart attack which brought a veil of fear to our lives. A hospital stay was required. There, another heart attack on May 6, 1992 placed Émile in the fragile domain between life and death. For 72 hours he hovered in ambiguity eluding the medical professionals. I stayed with him and with all my heart appealed to the Universal powers for his life. My reason for being, my dreams, my happiness, my very essence lay there attached to tubes and machinery. It was a living nightmare. Then, the vital energy stabilized in his body and Émile started on the road to recovery.

Our love and caring intensified and Émile was feeling healthy and well. We continued with our lives, hopes and dreams. I started to explore my long-time interest in healing and obtained my Diploma in Traditional Chinese Medicine and Acupuncture. I wanted to do everything in my power to assist and protect my soulmate.

However, the Universe had its plan which was not what we expected. On November 23, 1993 on the way to the movies, we stopped at Upper Canada Mall in Newmarket. There, on a bench, Émile died after another heart attack. Then, on December 5, 1993 Perdu was killed.

Pain engulfed me and the absurdity of everything became overpowering. Our home became my monastery. The pain tore me apart and yet in the depths of my being, I somehow knew this was not the end. I knew that love was a powerful energy that could not be destroyed. I knew that the bond I shared with Émile still existed and would always continue to exist. I knew that things had changed but that somehow Émile was still with me. I felt his love, his presence, and his caring.

This led me to explore the realms of life and death never wanting to succumb to any dogma. In my very personal, spiritual search guided by strong bonds of love, I read countless books. My search continues with a keen awareness that we are indeed "spiritual beings having a physical experience"; that death is a rebirth into another dimension; that bridges can be built between dimensions when love is strong; that love never dies.

What follows is a stream of reflections on our love.

The Beginning

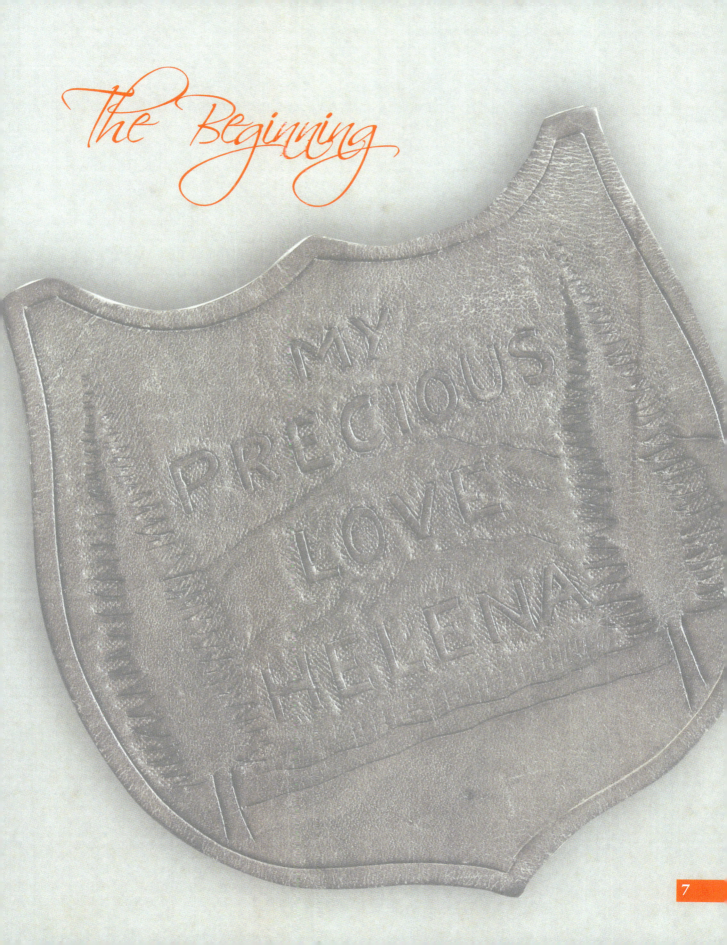

How strange and fascinating to look back at my life and recall the meandering path it followed through various experiences all unknowingly leading me to the ultimate experience of meeting my soulmate.

It was a gentle path of exciting opportunities, rewarding successes, unique travels and unexpected adventures. Wonderful people crossed my path. When others were not so kind and became a disappointment I always drew comfort and support from the endless bond of friendship of Teresa De Luca and Cathy Patel, and the limitless love of my parents.

I had a thirst for living and learning and a heart full of love. The beauty of Nature in all its exquisite forms marvelled me and I felt a deep awe for the mystery of the Universe. The age-old philosophical questions remained unanswerable but I knew, from an early age, that love was at the core of the meaning of life. I knew that to love and be loved by your soulmate was the ultimate goal and most meaningful experience of life. Back then I often looked out my bedroom window at a moonlit sky and knew that my love was out there somewhere perhaps looking at the same moon and stars. Whenever a wish was to be made, I always asked the Universe to lead me to my soulmate.

Personal and professional growth did not sway my conviction that a Great Love would appear. I was not anxious or worried as the days and seasons unfolded. Deep down within me I knew that it would happen, that it was meant to happen without my seeking it. I remained true to my inner knowing and confident that my heart would recognize that other soul, which would compliment mine. And so it happened.

One day Émile walked into my office and my world changed. I relive that moment with awe. All my steps through life and all his steps had led us to that place, to that moment. We had come from worlds apart. I had immigrated with my parents to Toronto from Portugal. His parents had emigrated from Ukraine to western Canada where he was born. Later he made his way to Toronto. Our lives had progressed toward each other, to be united and made whole. Like rivers meandering through space and time for a final reunion with the ocean, our souls had also arrived and in each other we found the boundless ocean of our love.

It was only a smile and friendly hello but his presence, his smile, his voice were engraved in my mind. It was a timeless moment, the beginning of a miracle. Gradually and relentlessly we recognized the soulmate in each other. The heart quickly acknowledged what reason took a bit longer to accept because reality often presents seemingly insurmountable obstacles to test our resolve.

In a world where doubt prevails, where scientific proof is of the utmost importance to explain phenomena, where the five senses determine reality, where the voice of reason speaks loudest, how do you explain the magic of love? There's a whole world of feelings, sensations, intuitive knowings that co-exist but can't be tapped within the confines of a materialistic world view. Here, love is felt and recognized and the voice of the heart is heard. Here too, impossible battles can be won and insurmountable obstacles overcome. The powerful energy of love helps us surface above the mundane and experience the flow of creation.

Although I lived in a world of reason, I inhabited the world of the heart when I met Émile. I listened to him and recognized my thoughts; I spoke and heard his words; I looked and saw gentleness and the depth of our love in his eyes. All that emerged from us merged together and wrapped us in a feeling of harmony and well-being.

My love for Émile became an absolute certainty, experienced in a simple act. He placed his hand behind my back to help me across the street. The energy that emanated from his touch made instant contact with every cell in my body and flooded my whole being. It was as if the core of me recognized and acknowledged the presence of my soulmate. This strong magnetic attraction stayed with us always and continues today.

Our souls knew we were meant to be together in spite of all odds. It would have been impossible to do otherwise because our lives were intertwined from time immemorial. I remember Émile's words, "I feel like I've known you for hundreds of years."

As we travelled the same path together, our horizons expanded. Our sense of freedom became greater as our mutual support helped us to explore hidden dimensions of ourselves. When we had different interests, we would pursue them with the encouragement of the other and return renewed and enriched to share our experiences. We became more creative and successful in our endeavours. We became more keenly aware of the world around us and its beauty. Every moment we shared was lived intensely. Our happiness at having found each other was palpable and sustained by the awe that such a miracle had happened to us.

Branded in my mind are countless moments of joy and wonder. I remember driving across the Canadian prairies when Émile suddenly stopped the car on the side of the road. We stepped out and he held me tightly and introduced me to the sound of the wind whispering through the tall grasses in the silence of the night. Always in tune with Nature he spotted wildlife when I least expected it.

Yes, there it was the wolf, the fox, the deer, the hawk … so many other creatures! I loved seeing the world through his eyes and later through his paintings.

His creative talents extended beyond painting to leather carving, wood work, architectural designs. He designed the plans for our home and built most of it alone. He wanted to build us a love nest and I contributed with love messages written on the wood frame.

His many skills amazed me and I loved to watch him during his creative process. Simple items such as a seashell, a piece of coral, a rock could be combined and transformed into a beautiful object. He saw the artistic potential of many things. He managed the brush, knife, pencil or hammer with the same dexterity and sensitivity.

But his sensitivity embraced everything he did. At work he was known for helping colleagues and clients and he was always ready to reach out and help a stranger. I remember a cold winter day when he brought home a poor fellow, he had picked up on the road, to share a hot meal with us. On another cold night he managed to bring home a frightened stray cat and then spent hours trying to befriend him until finally he was able to pick it up and bring it to me. It became our gentle, loving friend whom we named Perdu.

There were also many joyous moments spent together talking about everything – books, events, ideas, dreams … He was always there when I needed him to listen to my problems and worries. He helped me surface from the turmoil with a renewed perspective and sense of balance.

He brought me joy when we travelled and shared the excitement of new sights and experiences. I remember when we rented a motorcycle to explore the Moroccan desert; when we left our comfortable hotel in Cancun to stay in other parts of the Yucatan Peninsula so we could meet the local people; when we climbed a crumbling pyramid tucked away from the tourist sites in Mexico.

Always jovial and full of energy he would sweep me off my feet at the sound of dancing music. Whenever "The Power of Love" played he would drop everything to dance with me. Our bodies swayed fully aware of each muscle, each contour, seeking intimate contact, longing for the ultimate unity that only our kiss dared reveal.

The union of our souls and our bodies transported us to a realm of ecstasy and a direct communion with the divine. I always wanted to die that way because as soon as I was away from his arms, I missed him terribly.

Émile showed me heaven on earth and then he showed me heaven in the skies. I had never dreamed of flying beyond commercial flights. My passion was the ocean. It entranced me with its rhythm, its immensity, its many moods, its mystery, its tameless character and haunting call. A life on the ocean waves, sailing, free, was the vision that captured my imagination. I was fascinated by those who had done this like Robin Lee Graham and his sailboat, Dove.

Bernard Moitessier, another well known sailor, gave expression to my dream when he described sailing Joshua around the world in *La Longue Route*: "Les jours succèdent aux jours, jamais monotones. Même lorsqu'ils peuvent paraître exactement semblables, ils ne le sont jamais tout à fait. Et c'est cela qui donne à la vie en mer cette dimension particulière, faite de contemplation et de reliefs très simples. Mer, vents, calmes, soleil, nuages, oiseaux, dauphins. Paix et joie de vivre en harmonie avec l'univers."

" … les bruits de l'eau les bruits du vent, le chant de toutes les étoiles et de tous les soleils et de tous les clairs de lune ensemble, le combat et l'amour de l'homme et du bateau avec le vieil océan sur les vagues si grandes et les signes magiques venus du cœur profond de la mer profonde. …. La terre s'éloigne. Et maintenant c'est une histoire entre Joshua et moi, entre moi et le ciel, une belle histoire à nous tous seuls, une grande histoire d'amour qui ne regard plus les autres."

"…je rêve ma vie dans la lumière du ciel en écoutant la mer. "

I did not pursue a life on the ocean because Émile lifted my eyes to the sky. My first flight with him was in a Grumman Cheetah over the autumn landscape of Pennsylvania. The plane seemed to me a fragile toy defying the laws of gravity but the wings performed their magic and lifted us higher and higher. Then it was everything below us that appeared like toys. The brilliant colours of Fall created a masterpiece of this dwarf scenery. Our eyes were free to roam over towns, hills and valleys with unlimited visibility. This privileged vantage point, the freedom from earthly attachments and the thrill of speed was a new sensory experience for me. This was the dimension that Émile loved ever since he was a child. The fascination of watching birds in flight had led him to obtain his pilot's licence before he could drive a car.

He became transformed in the air, completely at one with his airplane, in deep concentration with his external and internal world; he was fully aware of all the details in his surroundings, silently rejoicing in the freedom of flight. Watching him I felt his serenity, admired his skill and was filled

with gratitude for being alive and sharing this world with My Love. As I leaned over to kiss his lips, we seemed suspended in space flooded by feelings unexpressed by words.

Émile was my constant source of inspiration. He had a positive outlook on life and an innate ability to erase obstacles instead of erecting them. His presence created a feeling of well-being and encouraged self-confidence. His enthusiasm dissipated all doubts and allowed dreams to emerge. His smile and words of encouragement ignited an inner driving force that led to action. What often seemed difficult and improbable became reality. In this atmosphere of love and support, I obtained my pilot's licence and began to share the left seat of our Grumman Traveller.

Before a flying trip we would toss a coin to determine who would be captain. During long cross-country flights, we took turns as pilot and navigator. These became memorable adventures across Canada and the United States.

It was wonderful to share the domain of all winged creatures. We felt small, insignificant and fragile before the lake dotted wilderness of northern Ontario; the imposing presence of the Rocky Mountains; the desolate expanses of Arizona and New Mexico deserts; the timeless grandeur of the Grand Canyon. Each scene was a masterpiece of such magnitude that the senses were too limited to capture and retain it. But our souls seemed to burst forth and embrace it all. We felt part of all of Nature, the Planet, the Sky, the Universe and we felt whole, we felt happy.

Our happiness extended to our daily lives. The problems, obstacles and frustrations we encountered were external to our own private world. Within our bubble of love everything between us flowed effortlessly. Even the trivial and mundane chores would be carried out by one of us with the intent of saving the other the trouble. Whenever Émile finished tasks first he would say, "Now we have more time for each other." Each of us was only concerned with giving to the other and in so doing we both received so much!

As I write I feel the failure of words to convey our feelings for each other. Émile often revealed in his love letters and poems the inadequacy of words to express his deep feelings for me but I intuited the ineffable.

This is only an iota of our love. Our passion will remain our secret.

The Change

15

*L*ife is a continuum of present moments. The salient ones transform us in profound ways. The moments I spent with Émile were the Mt. Everest of my life. Then came one sudden, unexpected, terrifying moment when Émile's life ebbed away plunging me into the desolate depths of the Mariana trench. That body that I had loved and caressed lay inert before me unresponsive, for the first time, to my touch. How could this be? Where was my Émile?

Raw pain tore at my insides and the chaos of confusion enveloped me. I watched without understanding and dissolved into tears embracing My Love. A primordial cry of agony and despair wanted to be released from the depths of my being but stayed silent within me as I realized that those around me would not accept or understand such behaviour. As it was they wanted to sedate me and take me away. I remember thinking, "How cruel can they be. Don't they know that my life lies there with My Love, that I've lost everything, that there's no other way to feel, that tears and pain are all I've left, that I don't want to be drugged to lull the emotions that I'm feeling, that all I want is to be alone with my Émile!"

At times like these one loses privacy and control over events. Society takes over to dictate what has to be done, when and where. This contributed considerably to my feelings of despair. I was forced to leave my Émile and go home alone. It was strange to notice how I was able to function (walk/talk/drive) even though the life force had abandoned my body. Everything around me seemed unreal, distant, absurd. The words of consolation from others seemed hollow, meaningless. Nothing could be said. I had nothing to say. I wanted to be alone.

My Émile, my life, my happiness, my joy, my passion had been sucked into the black hole of death. Why was my body still functioning?

I walked into the silence of our home. Perdu greeted me but there were no arms to hug me, lips to kiss me, tender voice to welcome me home. I searched all the rooms – empty! I was alone, dazed, wrapped in total disbelief. We had left our home not long ago to go to the movies. On the way we stopped at Upper Canada Mall in Newmarket. He held my hand for the last time. All the actions and words at that time and place were the last ones. It was there that it happened – not feeling well, sitting on a bench, collapsing. Everything became a whirl of my cries for help, of people, of holding my Émile,

of telling him that I loved him, of pleading for him to stay with me, of ambulance lights and sirens, hospital – the end.

As I paced through the house that night the same questions haunted me, "How is this possible? Where is my Émile? Why am I here without him?" Silence. Despair. More pain. Our friend Nick De Luca came. My brother George came. They were afraid to leave me alone. They wanted to help, like all my friends and relatives. But this was not within their power because they couldn't bring back my Émile.

The exposure to the strange, impersonal underworld of Funeral Homes plunged me deeper into absurdity. The staff wanted to proceed in a rational quiet manner to fill out papers, address details, make choices, prepare schedules. I looked astounded at the plastic expressions trained to repeat the same ritual without realizing that each individual death is unique and that a personal tragedy is unfolding for the loved ones.

I managed self control and serenity as they manoeuvered through the procedures and then I made two demands – no one was to touch my Émile, I would dress and prepare him; I would go with him to the crematorium. They were unwilling to forego the normal procedures but I found the strength to face them and to state firmly that it would be as I wanted.

How I longed to crawl into that coffin and sleep forever in my Émile's arms! How little time there was left to be with him! How much to ponder, to whisper to him! I was able to fill his pockets with love messages before a deluge of friends and relatives arrived. I heard their words of sorrow and support meant to help me but it was futile because Émile was beyond my grasp.

I did prepare my Émile and took my last ride with him to the crematorium. The staff tried to sneak away while I was surrounded by friends but I ran out and got into the hearse. I accompanied my Émile to his final destination and when they placed the coffin in the cremator, I pressed the button to start the flames. I didn't want a stranger to mindlessly carry out this last act. This was my Émile's last physical transformation and I was there with him. Throughout this whole nightmare I never said good-bye to Émile. I knew everything had changed but I felt he was still with me.

I experienced the collapse and transformation of my world. All joy, hopes and dreams had vanished. Our bubble of love had burst and I was faced with a world indifferent to my Émile's absence. Society continued in motion. People pursued their affairs. The sun continued to shine and birds to sing. This shocked me immensely. Surely the whole had to be affected when a part was missing. To me it was the most important part of the world – this beautiful human being no longer here to spread love, warmth, laughter. It seems that when a life is gone it's like a hole left in the sand which is quickly levelled off by the life force of the ocean and everything is as before. Only those who love deeply are permanently wounded by the hole left in their heart when death snatches the most important being in their life.

Friends and relatives continued to attempt to help me with well-intentioned words used again and again at times like these – "You have to accept that death is part of life. You have to forget and resume life. You have to join the world again, to socialize." None of their efforts had the intended effect on me. The constant question, "Are you better now?" puzzled me. Émile was still dead, how could I be better?

A great chasm opened up between others and myself. They couldn't fully understand the abyss of my pain and didn't know what else to say or how to act. My tragedy was beyond their frame of reference. I understood their frustration but I couldn't bridge the gap. Going back to the way things were, was impossible and moving forward into nothing was unthinkable. So I stood still, suspended in limbo and from there I watched the absurdity around me.

Crowds, noise, and commotion suffocated me and I would break into tears. Sights, sounds, smells and tastes that reminded me of Émile would trigger a flow of tears. My response to everything was tears. This was distressing to those close to me and I realized that my state was causing pain to others. The only solution was to hide the feelings and the tears. A great effort was required to accomplish this and I walked through the days in deep tiredness. My wholeness had disintegrated but others didn't see my shattered self. They thought they saw a whole being. My smile hid a silent cry.

I watched myself go through the motions of daily living, detached from life, and trapped in the heaviness of the physical body. The feeling of not belonging here overwhelmed me and I observed

the unfolding of events as if from a great distance. My senses were aware of my surroundings and I responded as a well-trained player but that wasn't me.

My interest was no longer in the material world. Previous desires for adventure, dreams of travelling and other plans just faded away. I felt a detachment from all previous longings and experienced a sense of relief. I didn't need to do anything or go anywhere – I just needed to be. In the silence of just being what surfaced were thoughts, feelings and sensations – in order to pursue these I needed to be alone.

My home became my sanctuary and I limited my ties to the external world – no phone, TV or computer. I remained accessible through personal contact and mail and was always open to assisting others but I became unable to deal with trivial interactions and social rituals. The importance of meaning in words and actions became vital to me.

I spent time reliving the details of the life I had shared with Émile, reading his letters and poems and looking through our photos. More powerful than the recollection of images and words was the love I felt for Émile. Death had not erased the feelings of the past or prevented present feelings from flowing with increased intensity. I continued to be conscious of Émile's energy around me. My frail being seemed to be bathed by his love. Death could not break the bond between us.

From that first night alone I became keenly aware of a presence, invisible to my senses, undefinable to my reason but real to my heart. As I opened myself to this experience, I felt Émile's love embracing me and I knew I was not alone. I desperately missed his physical presence, his touch, his smile, his voice, and all that he had been as a physical being but somehow I felt he was still with me. Dramatic personal experiences are often difficult to verbalize and share with others especially when people have definite views on everything including death. I chose to be silent because I had too much to say and words couldn't convey what was in my heart. I knew that most people would not understand or believe that there was anything exceptional for words to grasp.

I was seen as being at some stage of the grieving process that was taking longer than expected. People concerned with my being lonely, encouraged me again to go out, to be with others and do things. How could I explain that I was never lonely. The loneliness came in being with others who had erased

Émile from existence because they couldn't see or feel him. It came from others who hadn't known him or cared to know him even through me. I painfully felt their uneasiness when I brought him into a conversation. Their awkward smiles betrayed their discomfort when I talked about our life together.

They didn't know how to handle such situations and I felt the burden that I had become for them. Their silence became a barrier to communication. In reality there was little about which to communicate. They were immersed in their daily lives, dreaming, planning, acquiring, fulfilling their wishes. They lived in the world of their physical senses whereas I walked through life like a shadow, unsubstantial because I couldn't share it with Émile in the same way.

It took endless energy to try to show interest in the mundane, to smile and appear pleasant. People don't like sadness or tragic figures. They shun anything that upsets their world, their views, their sense of order. I tried to be friendly and receptive to those who crossed my path but I couldn't deny Émile's existence. How could I talk about myself without mentioning him? The I in me contained him. We were inseparable. So I kept tripping over their uneasiness and almost had to excuse myself for being.

When your world is knocked off its axis and your orbit becomes different from everyone else's, it is easiest to be alone. It was not their fault but it was not my fault either. A change had occurred, a transformation which affected me deeply. To deny this and attempt to be normal would mean to become untruthful to myself in order to fit into other people's expectations.

The closeness I felt to Émile and the flow of love between us reinforced our relationship. Deep down within me I knew that our love could never be destroyed; that new ways of relating could be found; that new levels of awareness could be activated. A new path was before me. In order to proceed I had to suspend my rational self. I had to explore a different realm of existence beyond the prison of our physical senses. I felt compelled to reach out to Émile. I felt sure that if I kept an open heart, my intuitive self would guide the way.

The Driving Force

With Émile's death began my rebirth into a new level of awareness. I felt that our love was the key to help me penetrate the veil between us. My heart and my intentions were pure and my attempt to reach out was fearless. In quietude I waited eagerly to receive a sign that I was on the right path. A powerful wave of love engulfed me and my heart throbbed as I walked through the days with a sense of purpose.

I began to let go of even the smallest plans and expectations and to allow myself to flow with whatever happened. I searched for the hidden lesson or message in each event and began to understand that nothing happens by chance or without a purpose. At the centre of everything there is a lesson to be unwrapped. An energy greater than the self guides us through the school of life whenever we are willing to be open and receptive to our inner voice. Each time we follow it we experience a sense of comfort and well-being. Our false sense of control and importance blocks the link with this greater energy and we stumble through life gaining little from our experiences.

There was an incredible sense of freedom and adventure in following my footsteps without deciding on the path. They often led me to encounters with the natural world where its creatures became the messengers. Animals don't speak our language but they are part of the same whole as we. When our paths cross we can choose to ignore them or to stop and ponder on the purpose of the encounter. Their appearance communicates something, if we take the time to decipher it.

With Émile forever centred in my thoughts, I searched for signs to confirm his presence. On a tree branch outside our living room window stood a hawk (the first and only time). We looked at each other as if mesmerized and then I felt a surge of love invading me. As it flew away I knew something had been revealed.

We had always found the chickadees very endearing but too skittish to afford a close encounter. They had been one of the subjects of Émile's paintings and reminded me of times we had spent together watching them. One day, their twittering sound led me outside to the mountain ash tree where they seemed to be feasting. As usual they fanned out as I approached, but this time there was one exception. A chickadee allowed my close proximity and I saw his beady little eyes

looking at me unafraid. Tears came to my eyes. I felt love rushing through me and once again I was grateful.

A pair of Canada geese have faithfully nested in our backyard every year. Canada geese mate for life and Émile once painted the lovers in flight. I thought it was romantic to have them share our space and symbolize our love. This made my next gift also very special. I was clearing leaves along the road in front of the house when I saw at the bottom of a pile two goose feathers side by side in perfect condition in spite of all the debris around them. It was a magic moment because I knew with a deep certainty that this was a gift from my Émile. Countless other episodes followed. During my many solitary walks I was enthralled when I came across rocks in the shape of hearts, which to me spoke his silent words of love.

Another memorable moment – I cried as I followed a country road where we used to go for walks. I relived the laughter and talks we had shared; the stolen hugs and kisses; the joy of receiving his bouquet of wildflowers; the warmth of his hand and of the love we felt for each other. The acute pain of missing him kept the tears flowing and I longed for his presence. Out of nowhere a red-winged black bird came swooping over my head, turned and flew ahead of me. Startled I watched as he came back to repeat the same pattern for the duration of my walk. He was a reminder that I was not alone and I smiled.

The magic of each situation lies in feeling the contact, in being touched in your heart and knowing the message. The limits of language make it difficult to share the opening of these new doors. At the level of the rational mind it all amounts to interesting coincidences with no proof of anything substantial. But the rational mind offers no understanding of magic or even love. And love does exist, so does magic!

Increasingly I felt that death was not the end, was not oblivion, was not nothing. A physical disintegration occurred but something else happened. I couldn't visualize or fully understand what or how it happened but the stirrings of a long forgotten sense confirmed that there was continuity.

One thought kept haunting me – ice changing to water and water to steam. The same element in different states depending on the vibratory level of its molecules. From the tangible to the elusive. From the physical to the ethereal. From the visible to the invisible yet still there in a different form, not lost. An ancient voice within reminded me that death was a change, not a loss, not an absence, but a transformation.

Yes, Émile, you are still here. Not just in my mind, in my memories of you but present beside me, in me, around me. Your energy is real, your love is real and interacts with me at every moment everywhere. This is not something to be proven to others but to be experienced directly. There are no physical references to enable others to understand. There are no words to convey the feeling. It is beyond the physical experience of everyday life. But this does not mean that it is not real. It is a different level of reality.

There were many, many intense experiences that rewarded my existence but did not diminish my craving for Émile's physical presence. I wore and continue to wear his shirts and sweaters in order to recapture his cozy hug and tender touch.

My interactions with people became less tearful (I was able to keep the tears to myself). I carried on a conversation and did what needed to be done but all along I ached for Émile and sought him in the beyond. I was only half present because I was only half there.

Often I watched outside of myself – me and life all around. I watched people's experiences: how certain situations kept recurring in different disguises with the same lessons embedded in them; how the same mistakes kept being repeated without their awareness; how the same cycle of emotions kept surfacing because people kept stumbling over the same obstacles. I saw the simplicity of the lesson and the difficulty in the learning. I was also a player in this game of life. From somewhere outside of myself I watched my struggle, my stumbles and falls. I watched myself trying to learn, trying to emerge, trying to unfold my invisible wings for an eternal flight.

While alone it was easiest to maintain a focus on the present moment to sharply observe and acutely listen. By letting go of attachments to predetermined outcomes I was able to open my being to the

Universe and follow the dictates of my heart. This way I became more aware of my Émile's presence and more receptive to the guidance I was being given.

The challenge for me was transferring this state of being to everyday situations. External noise made it difficult to maintain internal silence and to listen. Diversions were an obstacle to awareness and seeing. Pressures and problems shifted the focus from the heart to the mind. I felt trapped in a crowd, unable to surface with serenity and centredness. All of society seemed to conspire against this new state of being I had discovered.

It took me awhile to realize that society was as it had always been. The change was in me and I had to learn to find the silence and to listen in the midst of noise; to maintain awareness and to see through the diversions; to follow my heart under all circumstances; to protect my space within a crowd; to remain serene and centred at all times; to maintain the bond with the Universe and my Émile in spite of everything. This challenge continues before me. Some days I'm better able to maintain the balance than others. Whenever I falter I feel my Émile's love embracing me, giving me the courage to try again.

My Émile's departure from physical reality opened a spiritual door to endless learnings and insights and in a radically different way led to a greater proximity between us.

The Quest

My desire to learn more about the fundamental questions of life and death led me to revisit the world of religion and philosophy. I read in earnest trying to find something that rang true in my heart.

Organized religions seem to offer a pre-packaged set of rules, observances and codes of behaviour for their followers. Faith and beliefs are the common foundations to all and call for acceptance without questioning. Intermediaries are required to bridge the real and spiritual worlds. Little attention or encouragement is given to individual direct spiritual experience.

The mystical traditions provide more meaningful insights into spiritually significant occurrences. Also, the teachings of the masters of the Far East speak of different levels of reality; of knowledge beyond reasoning; of the interconnectedness of all things; of personal journeys beyond the material world. This had a special appeal for me because of the shift from the orbit of beliefs to direct experience.

My previous contacts with Aboriginal Peoples had introduced me to Shamanism and I was drawn to that worldview where man, Nature and its creatures are spiritually connected and able to communicate; where different levels of reality co-exist and can be explored; where the spirit world can be accessed to enhance knowledge and achieve healing. This is another tradition that encourages first hand experience of non-ordinary reality and is devoid of dogma. Exploring shamanic methods has given me many rewarding experiences.

The world of philosophy, specifically western philosophy, dwells in the realm of the intellect and draws on logic and reasoning to seek insights. Although, in the past, I had wandered through the halls of the great minds of humanity, I now experienced a need far greater than intellectual stimulation.

I was driven to explore another level of reality and thus I stumbled on quantum physics. It was fascinating to discover that scientists are moving beyond the common concepts of classical physics because these are too limited to describe Nature. The subatomic world of their studies

reveals matter as a form of energy in continual motion and change. Science is disclosing a world where everything is connected, flows and changes. Quantum reality is not accessible to the ordinary senses but it exists. Invisibility does nor mean non-existence. A major obstacle to moving beyond sensory perception is the rational mind that seeks proof and tries to use physical tools to test the non-physical.

I've learned that one must keep an open mind and be non-judgmental before the mysteries of the Universe. I have also learned that the lessons from direct experience with the non-physical must be lived, they can't be taught.

It's a process of following an inward drive, listening to the voice within, the intuitive self. It requires staying in tune with what feels right and true from the essence of our being. It implies being willing to forge alone knowing that you are not alone.

My Émile's love became the driving force that opened me to the guidance of the Universe. By allowing things to happen I soon found that I would be guided to specific books. I was compelled to read them and sometimes wondered why until I came across a specific sentence or phrase of great relevance to me. It was like finding a hidden jewel. The same thing happened with situations and people. I was enthralled with the experience of letting go and flowing with whatever happened.

One day I walked into a bookstore, followed my steps and stopped before a book – *Reunions* by Dr. Raymond Moody. It was the last one on the shelf. For some reason my heart started to beat faster and then I saw that this book was about "visionary encounters with departed loved ones".

I had read all of Dr. Moody's books on near-death experiences and regression hypnosis and found his research fascinating and encouraging. His findings suggested the existence of life after death and so did my own experience with Émile.

I wanted to pursue more active communication with Émile and perhaps contact. I wasn't sure whether this would be possible but I had been led to Dr. Moody's latest book where he presented more research to confirm that the living could commune with departed loved ones.

Later, when I met Dr. Moody during one of his lecture tours, I was again encouraged by his open mindedness, his warm personality and his dedication to exploring a field that has been neglected and frowned upon by most medical professionals. His scientific research has given legitimacy to these paranormal experiences but it's an individual's direct experience and insight that result in personal transformation.

Reunions was the Universe's message that I would be able to contact Émile. As I hungered for this to happen, my inner voice told me, "Be Patient. When the fruit is ripe it will fall."

There are many tools/methods that have been used throughout the ages for divination and to communicate with "the other side" such as *The I Ching*, Tarot, Ouija, automatic writing, dowsing, scrying. Each can be a door to many insights if the user's intentions are driven by a real desire/need to connect and learn. Many times we seek specific, clear answers but what is received are guidelines, food for thought that trigger the inner knowing.

Each method requires much effort and dedication for effective use. I explored these venues on my own but also through intermediaries. While resorting to a professional, such as a Tarot reader, can be a fascinating experience, it can create a dependency factor. Also, there is the danger of becoming a sponge and absorbing everything that is being interpreted. I stumbled through these obstacles and learned that the Universe often tests us to see if we are alert and listening to our heart or just blindly accepting a reading.

The old saying "When the student is ready the master appears" gained a special meaning for me when Lynne Scarlett introduced me to a very spiritual human being , Doug Gray. Immediately, I felt a strong bond with this person full of ancient wisdom. With kindness and patience I was guided in establishing a clearer communication link with Émile and the Universe.

Certain factors were key in my quest: my clarity of purpose and positive intention driven by my love for Émile; my trust in the Universe as a source of love that permeates everything; my fearless pursuit; my openness to a reality beyond the senses. My major learning involved listening. When thoughts are silenced and we are in tune with the Universe, guidance flows into us without the need of tools. We are told what we need to know not necessarily what we want to know. The school of life is for learning and most things we must discover on our own. I discovered that love is the most important thing in life and beyond. My relationship with Émile continues because our love was able to bridge the mystery that separates us. And in the silence within me his words of love flood my being and give me the strength to face each day.

As I flow along my path new experiences arise and fill me with wonder. And so I wait patiently for the ultimate experience of a reunion.

The Last Steps

The radical change in my life has led me to become more of an observer than a participant in the play of life. It's not indifference that prevents my involvement but a feeling of separateness. This has enhanced my awareness and perception of life and my body seems too limited to contain all that I feel.

It's difficult to give full expression to my passion for the ocean. It hypnotizes me with its motion, its call. When I step into the foamy waters and walk forward to meet its heartbeat, the water rises around my body, accepts my intrusion and embraces me. I'm lifted to stretch over its surface and ride the waves. Swimming to the crest of a wave, I only see the sky ahead and feel the sensation of taking off into the unknown. Effortlessly, I plunge down into the trough only to be lifted again by the following wave. I feel the freedom of a fish or a bird. Out there alone I feel detached from the physical world. It's not always a roller coaster ride. Sometimes the water is placid and only the swimming motion disturbs the stillness, cutting through the mirror image of the sky. Whenever I merge with the ocean, I feel joy and gratitude.

There were many other things that I used to love to do, such as horseback riding, flying, dancing, travelling. These activities gave rise to multiple emotions savoured from being at one with the horse, the plane, the music, the world. Now I love the memory of how it used to be and the idea of becoming these things in all their emotional expressiveness.

People find it odd that I don't have the urge to travel like I once did. There's stimulating energy, something appealing about the notion of departing, leaving to go elsewhere. In the past, the physical destination held all the excitement with the promise of new sights, people, adventure. Now, the notion of departing takes on a greater sense, a transition to a new dimension. Leaving without arriving. Beyond all horizons. To be in the Undefinable. To merge with my Émile. In love. Forever.

I follow the flow of each day without plans or expectations and although I'm isolated in a little corner of the world and "alone" I have been on a great journey of discovery, a journey I was compelled to make. My learnings far surpass those of all my physical travels.

As I walk along my path, I know that before my departure, there is a purpose to be fulfilled which unfolds with each step. In my sphere of contacts with others, I try to be useful and assist to lighten their burdens or enhance their joy. A contribution of love is always useful towards the balance of the whole.

In all human development nothing is static and fluctuations often accompany the process of change. I always strive to find my centre and be serene in each present moment. However, there are times when this eludes me. My Émile's love always rescues me and I start anew.

I don't know when my final steps will end but I would like to determine how the cycle will be closed. If possible I would like to take my last breath sitting on the bench where my Émile made his transition. The bench was donated and delivered to our home by the management of Upper Canada Mall in Newmarket when I requested to purchase it. I was haunted by the need to have it and am grateful it has been with me since then.

When I die I do not want any funereal procedures or rites. I wish to be left as I am and cremated in the simplest coffin. I want to take my Émile's photo which I have carried every day and night since his departure. Also a leather crest which Émile carved for me with "My Precious Love, Helena." I would like a reading of the poems *High Flight* by John Gillespie Magee Jr., and *Reflection of Love* by B.E. Stefel, which were also read at Émile's funeral. For a musical farewell, Albinoni's Adagio and Jennifer Rush's *The Power of Love*.

My final request is for my ashes and my Émile's ashes to be released together from a plane over the ocean. The wind will blow away our last physical remains and we will become an iota of the ocean but only Émile and I will ever know the extent of our love.

The Poems

The following
are modest poems
of my pain, anguish, search
and the undying love
between myself and Émile.
They are cries straight from the heart.

I Will Always *Love You Émile*

Two months have gone by
Since that fatal day in November
And people are still wondering why
I still remember.

"Are you better now?"
They ask, afraid to find
That my pain somehow
Will make me lose my mind.

"All our lives progress
Towards the inevitable end
Don't let your thoughts regress
To something you can't mend."

"Face reality you must
And walk along your path.
To deny destiny is unjust
Life must end in death."

Words meant to heal
A broken heart, an empty shell
But none can really feel
The pain in my every cell.

I Miss You

You and I alone
Happy and in love
Together we made a home
A nest for our love.

Then destiny placed
Perdu on our way
And the three of us faced
Happily each day.

To us life was kind
We always showed we cared
Our love was our greatest find
I was so happy it made me scared.

Suddenly it all came to an end
I still can't believe it's true
That now I must stand
All alone without you.

Across the great divide you flew
And left us all alone
This was too much for little Perdu
And he followed to your new home.

Together I hope you now are
In some place of bliss
Someday I will travel that far
Until then you both I will miss.

Unforgettable Feeling

The energy of your touch
The warmth of your hand
It was powerful and too much
For me to understand.

This first time I felt and knew
Being touched by grace
That this serenity with you
Came from a previous time and place.

And each time your hand
Caressed or touched me, somehow
I began to understand
The power of our past in the now.

The energy that flowed
Through our beings in touch
Remained in me and showed
How I loved you so much.

You too couldn't explain
The power that drew
Us together to remain.
It was timeless the love we knew.

This love, this passion
Lifted us beyond reality
To surpass mortal attraction
And envelop us with awe and humility.

Too powerful to deny
We knew it had to be
Our Love had to cry
Its glory to Eternity.

Loving You Always

Your look, your smile
Your tender words too
Made me stop and stay awhile
And fall in love with you.

Your care and tenderness
Your understanding too
All this and your caress
Made me fall in love with you.

Your support and affection
Your encouragement too
Gave your love expression
And I fell in love with you.

For your respect and trust
For believing in me too
For all this and more I must
And will always love you.

Is it you?

A breeze over my face
Is it you, Émile
Giving me an embrace?

Are you still here with me?
Is it you I feel?
I need to know, I need to see.

I don't know why
The sensation is so real
There are no answers and I cry.

Why?

Why did you have to go?
Tell me, my Love
Do you now know?

I can't understand, I can't accept
You were just here
And suddenly you left.

So much yet to do and see
Dreams to dream
For you and me.

Now my broken heart in pain
Cries out for you
Only its echo and silence remain.

 but Pain

I relive the past
All in my mind
It went so fast
But to us was kind.

To others I talk
Lost in disbelief
Alone I walk
Deep is my grief.

I need you Émile
To be whole again
Otherwise I'll feel
Nothing but pain.

Searching

I read and read
To learn and find out
What Life and Death
Are all about.

My mind must grow
And learn to see
Other places and dimensions
Where you must be.

I must study and learn
How the veil to part
That separates our world
Keeping us apart.

I must transcend
Earthly vibrations
And learn to feel
Spiritual sensations.

This and much more
I'll learn to do
So I can always be
In touch and near you.

First Spring Day *Without You*

The sun's rays kissed
The blanket of snow
And the earth we missed
Underneath began to show.

The sky was blue
Not a cloud in sight
Along the path without you
I walked in fright.

T'was the fear of seeing
The awakening of Spring
And knowing in my being
That my heart could never sing.

Other bodies walked
The same path as I
They smiled and talked
Not hearing my sigh.

T'was the voice of my heart
Calling for you in pain
But knowing from the start
It was all in vain.

You could not reply
To my aching heart so broken
And I started to cry
Longing to hear your love spoken.

You were inside me
Walking along that path
But I still longed to see
You, even after death.

I missed your presence so much
Holding hands too
I longed for your touch
And sharing Spring with you.

Time is Slow *Without You*

The days flow one into the other
Without meaning or reason
The future becomes the present but I don't bother
As winter gives way to another season.

I sleep, eat and talk
I am still alive to the outside
But I've lost the desire to take a walk
The joy and happiness I felt by your side.

In the depths of me
Emptiness and pain prevail
I've lost the desire to explore, to see
To travel, to fly or sail.

I am a body without a soul
That, you took with you
Being in your arms is my only goal
I have to wait until my life is through.

Our life together went so fast
Yet now all is so slow
I dwell in the past
And will never let go.

The Pain of Your Absence

The robins are back
Other birds too
But your love I lack
And the presence of you.

Their songs fill the air
But my heart can't rejoice
I feel it's not fair
That I can't hear your voice.

Spring breezes brush away
Winter's carpet of snow
But in my heart it'll stay
And cold winds will blow.

In my soul there's sadness
Which fills me inside
Others think it's madness
My feelings I must hide.

The hour is not yet here
For me to go into the Light
Lessons to learn are not clear
So I continue with my plight.

It's a very strange sensation
Living alone without you
It's beyond explanation
And comprehension too.

Tears often come
To relieve the pain in me
From others I must run
So my grief they won't see.

"Time will make it pass
Time will be the cure
What you need is time to elapse
Of that you can be sure."

They can't understand or know
Our timeless love unbroken
And those words only show
That my pain can't be spoken.

Reaching out

Five months and five days ago
You stepped into the Light
Since then time seems slow
As each day turns into night.

The days are hard to face
As endless demands are made of me
The nights protect my own space
As I try to join you in Eternity.

I open my being to the Universe
I close my eyes and meditate
I hope with you to converse
In this or any altered state.

Our bonds will never be broken
But I must find a way
To hear your love spoken
And communicate with you someday.

We Are One

You dwell in me
And I in you
We're both alive and dead
Here and There
But most of the time
Caught
In-between.

Heart, Why did You Stop Beating?

Your heart of gold
Full of love for me
Held our secrets of old
So no one else could see.

I would lie on your chest
And hear its faithful beat
Thus I loved to rest
Till it lulled me to sleep.

Then on the third of May
It made us quite scared
And on the sixth day
Leave you it almost dared.

It was a nightmare
It was insane
It was my greatest scare
And left my heart in pain.

Then time began to heal
That gold heart of yours
And we both began to feel
The opening of new doors.

You were doing well
Buoyed by a new tide
But we couldn't really tell
What was going on inside.

Often I would ask
Your heart to be good
Not to beat too fast
And behave as it should.

You would smile at me
As I spoke to your heart
In your eyes I could see
The love it stored from the start.

But the nightmare was to return
And fill me with fright
As your heart decided to run
From you on that November night.

It left without a good-bye
And stopped its faithful beat
Leaving me alone to cry
Never to lull me to sleep.

They Don't Understand

To others it's a closed chapter

Helena and her Émile

It's over and it doesn't matter

Or impact on how they feel.

Some who haven't found

A soulmate to love and cherish

Are puzzled and frown

On a love that can't perish.

Impatient with my state

Of remembrance and pain

They tell me it was fate

And from sadness there's no gain.

No words can ever convey

A love that transcends Time and Space

So I leave them and go my way

To follow a different tune and pace.

We Are *Still Together*

With every breath

I'll think of you forever

And relive the path

Of our lives together.

Our feelings were so intense

Our bonds so strong

Our love so immense

Our life together not long.

You're still here

In the midst of me

Your thoughts I hear

Though you I cannot see.

Your energy I feel

Vibrating in my being

To me this is real

And only I know the feeling.

There Must Be *A Way*

Destiny our future stole
Our dreams came to an end
In this reality I'm no longer whole
And Space and Time I must learn to bend.

A bridge within me
To reach you in some way
This I seek desperately
And hope to find it someday.

To master the mind
To concentrate
To leave behind
The normal state.

I must try and remember
What perhaps we all once knew
And learn to surrender
To the wisdom of the chosen few.

In the depths of our mind
The knowledge is stored but blocked
From them the key I must find
And open the doors that have been locked.

Searching *For You*

I call "Émile!" out loud
To hear your name
But all is silent like a shroud
Nothing will ever be the same.

You don't answer when I call you
In despair I sit down and cry
I only hear my echo calling through
The empty house and a buzzing fly.

I run upstairs and plan to sneak
Behind you as you paint
Into your creation I want to peek
But the empty room leaves me faint.

Perhaps you went out and soon I'll hear
"Tweetie, I'm home!"
But instead again comes the fear
Of knowing I'm all alone.

The Flame of Our Love

With graceful and passionate hands
The flames undress
The log that now stands
Naked under their caress.

In their passionate love making
With whispers and cries
The flames and log are taking
Our shape in my eyes.

I feel your warmth, your touch
Your loving tenderness, the bliss
Your lips that I love so much
Sealing our ecstasy with a kiss.

The heart beat of Creation
Is felt within our soul
And we experience the sensation
Of being one with the Whole.

The flames and log continue to dance
In the fireplace before me
As I come out of my trance
And with you long to be.

I miss you here in the now
To hold me close to you
And thus I try somehow
To relive the love we once knew.

The flame of our love will burn
Forever in my memory
Until it's time to return
To you in Eternity.

"The Power of Love"

"The Power of Love", our song
To its rhythm we'd sway
And feel our love so strong
That in each other's arms we'd stay.

Falling in love with you
Each day and each night
Was the reality I knew
An ongoing magical flight.

"I'm your lady and you're my man"
Don't ever forget these words of the song
And that I'm yours and you can
Reach out because to you I belong.

"Lost is how I'm feeling"
This is so very true
And from the depths of my being
I long to be with you.

"I'm headed for somewhere I've never been"
To look for you without fear
A place I have never seen
But must find to have you near.

The journey is hard and it may be long
"But I'm ready to learn about the power of love"
How it makes us determined and strong
With a little help from Above.

In Search *of* Balance

I find my centre
In your warm embrace
I find my centre
And wipe the tears off my face.

I find my centre
In the essence of you
I find my centre
In our love so true.

I find my centre
In the smile in your eyes
I find my centre
But my heart still cries.

I find my centre
In your passionate kiss
I find my centre
But your lips I miss.

I find my centre
In your poems to me
I find my centre
In how life used to be.

I find my centre
In our wings up high
I find my centre
But I break down and cry.

I find my centre
In all we have been
I find my centre
In my stillness within.

I find my centre
In all that you do
I find my centre
In my love for you.

I find my centre
And pray
In balance to stay
Until my dying day.

Deeds of Love

Love from you flowed
And in everything you did it showed
As you tried with so much might
To diminish other people's plight.

I remember:

One cold winter day you came home sneezing
Your hands without gloves freezing
Because you had given them away
To a lonely man you picked up on the highway.

I remember:

On the road you met another lonely soul
And brought him home for a hot soup bowl
You shared your warmth and your food
And he said he had never felt so good.

I remember:

The cashier rang in the items and placed them in a bag
The old lady without enough money looked sad
As she tried to decide which items to put away
You stepped forward and told the cashier you'd pay.

I remember:

The barefoot kid begging in the street
You took to a restaurant and bought him something to eat.
And the countless things you'd do and say
To bring some sun into each person's day.

At work you were known for going the extra mile
In helping others always with a smile.
Many were the letters of thanks you received
You did it all because in love and kindness you believed.

Shamanic *Journey*

With the Fox as my guide
I descend into the tree
And along its roots I slide
Until a clearing I see.

There, an old man meditates
Underneath the intertwined root dome
Where a burning fire illuminates
What must be his home.

The Fox whispers in his ear
The reason for my intrusion
He tells me to lie down and have no fear
Because reality is an illusion.

To the sound of his voice
My being floats away from within me
It feels calm, this is my choice
It leaves my gross body so I can be free.

It finds an exit through the ceiling
To a sunny Spring meadow
Where my smoke like being
First sees the Eagle in a shadow.

Its penetrating eyes read my mind
As its black feathers I caress
The Eagle knows it's you I want to find
And is willing my wish to address.

I climb on its back
Its wings thrust into the air
I hold on and embracing its neck
I feel the wind blowing through my hair.

Through layers of clouds we fly
Into space out of sight
The Eagle continues and doesn't ask why
I must visit you in the Light.

Over the edge of a silver cloud
Flowers bloom in a country scene
The Eagle lands gently and is proud
To show me this place so serene.

I sense a presence and then I see
Undefinable shapes bathed in light
You emerge walking towards me
And I'll never forget that sight.

"Tweetie, what are you doing here?"
I feel your words in my heart
Then it's the drum beat I hear
Calling me back to the journey's start.

The Eagle is restless ready to fly
And in a whirlpool of speed and sound
We leave in a hurry without a good-bye
The beat leads us homeward bound.

The speed increases with each beat
The pull of gravity is immense
We arrive at the old man's retreat
Where my body waits and feels tense.

My being slips into my body and I stand
Thanking my friends I start to leave
Without words we understand
That all this is hard to believe.

I follow the Fox out of the tree
Through the same route we took
The drum stops, I open my eyes and see
I'm home and beside me is the Shaman's Book.

The senses are limited to explain
The many realities that co-exist
We can ignore and from them refrain
Or be open, explore and persist.

The body is trapped in this reality
The soul's freedom has no bounds
I'll follow to achieve affinity
With you through images or sounds.

When love is strong and intentions are pure
We can learn our energies to align
Death is a rebirth, of this I'm sure
We are part of the Universe's Great Design.

The Mystery

The mystery of Creation
Has been with us from the start
But it's revelation
Is only accessed through the heart.

Reason pursues tasks
For knowledge acquisition
But knowledge knowing masks
And this leads not to fruition.

The unfeeling realms of the mind
Reason all but fail
Creation's answers to find
And the Mystery to unveil.

The flow of love from the heart
Is the Mystery's key
To be nurtured from the start
And allow us all to see.

Love like a flower can penetrate
The concrete of the unfeeling mind
Its petals can open if we concentrate
To reveal the answers we longed to find.

Like a flood of energy
Too powerful to contain
Love can burst forth in its majesty
To enfold all and claim its domain.

The spark of Creation
Only through love do we feel
It's a divine sensation
When love breaks the mystery's seal.

Our love is the key
To all this and more
All who listen to their hearts can see
The treasures love has in store.

They Will Never Understand

This aching pain
Forever constant in me
Is impossible to explain
To those I see.

Time moves on in their mind
And they can't understand
When they speak to me and find
That in the past is where I stand.

In daily reality and idle chatter
It's strenuous to participate
I try hard but it doesn't matter
If I can't communicate.

Judgements and opinions are made
Of my solitary life
New ones emerge as old ones fade
Ignorant of my deep strife.

I understand and don't mind
How can they possibly know
What it is like to find
A love like you and then let go.

Yin and Yang Separated

On the past I lean
Where my heart once sang
I am yin
And have lost my yang.

You are the vigor, the warmth, the light
The yang of my soul
Without you it's a cold dark night
With only yin I'm not whole.

Yin and yang in balance need to be
Intertwined and together
For life to smile in harmony
In this dimension and forever.

You Know When *It's Love*

How do you know? They ask
How can you tell the love is real?
Isn't it an impossible task?
No, I tell them, You can feel.

It's easy to know

When you don't have to ask
When you can bare your soul
When you don't need any mask
When your heart beats out of control.

It's easy to know

When all your being tingles
When the world shines and glows
When Earth with Heaven mingles
When only love from you flows.

It's easy to know

When you see a fairy in the firefly
When you see magic all around
When the beauty of Nature makes you cry
When you hear music in every sound.

It's easy to know

When bliss from Above descends
When the wind and trees to you speak
When your soul reality transcends
When other shores you need not seek.

It's easy to know

When you can feel the Universe vibrating
When you can touch the stars above
When you can feel your heart pulsating
Then you know it's love, it's love!

You can tell
When love is real
There's a spell
You can feel.

Isn't it so, Émile?

A Place *for Us*

The corridors of Time and Space
I search and feel lost
But I must find our Place
No matter what the cost.

I know there must be
A Shangri-la for two
A special Place for you and me
Where skies are brilliant blue.

Where the ocean kisses the sand
With fervour and might
Where flowers bloom and mountains stand
Where animals roam without fright.

Where the wind conducts a symphony
Where birds and brooks whisper their song
Where all of Nature lives in harmony
That's where you and I belong.

I know this must be so
Our love will open the door
Beyond this dimension we'll go
To love and embrace as before.

My Love For You Grows

My love for you grows
In every atom of every cell
It floods my being and it shows
That I'm under its spell.

Where are the words to express
My love, my joy, my song
All the feelings that I possess
And that to you belong.

Love is energy and power
Strong as steel
Gentle as a flower
This we know and feel.

As the ocean meets the shore
Towards you my life flows
To merge with you forevermore
This love that grows and grows.

With Gratitude To

Universal Love and Guidance forever present in my life.

Émile C. Klinowski who gives meaning, love and passion to my life.

The Klinowski family for sharing Émile with me.

My parents, Julio and Armanda Guerreiro, for their ever-present love and guidance and for having given me the opportunities to pursue my path.

My brother and sister-in-law, George and Maureen Guerreiro, who graciously named their daughter, Olivia Émiley, after Émile.

My uncle and aunt, Orlando and Rosa Rafael, who have given me much love and support. They flew from the U.S. to rush to my side during the most critical moment of my life.

Teresa De Luca, my loving childhood friend, who exited this world on February 20, 1993. She was always available to listen, support and assist whenever I needed her.

Cathy Patel, whose friendship is precious, has shared many phases of my life and continues to understand me better than anyone. Her professionalism and dedication enabled the publication of this book.

Doug and Fran Gray, my dearest friends from many lifetimes, whose spiritual guidance was the key that opened many doors for me.

Fred Case, an outstanding University of Toronto professor and dear friend, who always inspired me. He sadly passed away on May 10, 2008.

Christine Turkewych, my loyal friend and colleague, who during my darkest hours managed to bring me down to earth long enough for me to complete management training commitments and the co-authorship of our second training manual.

Deborah Levine, a long time friend, who has maintained her constant support in spite of her busy life.

Estelle Reed, my friend of many years, who has taught me many valuable lessons.

Deborah Rinzler who has experienced a similar tragedy in her life and shared her path with me.

Lynne Scarlett who entered our lives to become a bridge to fascinating discoveries.

Friends too numerous to mention who continue to give me love and support.

Perdu and Carlo, my four legged friends, who always gave me so much unconditional love.

21796676R00061

Made in the USA
Lexington, KY
28 March 2013